CHELSEA
FOOTBALL CLUB
Official Annual 2025

Written by Richard Godden and Dominic Bliss
Designed by Adam Wilsher

A Grange Publication

© 2024. Published by Grange Communications Ltd., Edinburgh, under licence from Chelsea FC Merchandising Limited. www.chelseafc.com.

Printed in the EU.

ISBN 978-1-915879-80-6

Welcome

Welcome to The Official Chelsea FC Annual 2025, packed full of stories, games, stats, facts and insight from those in the know at Stamford Bridge.

Discover the back stories to our new men's and women's team managers, Enzo Maresca and Sonia Bompastor, and find out what makes elite players like Cole Palmer and Lauren James tick.

We look at the new arrivals at the Bridge and look back on the good times with some of the heroes who departed in the summer, such as Thiago Silva, Fran Kirby and Emma Hayes.

Plus we take a look at the latest young ballers coming out of the Academy.

There's plenty of history too, in a season packed full of anniversaries for legendary moments that have gone down in Blues folklore. You'll discover how we won our first Premier League title 20 years ago, in 2004/05, and how we took the WSL crown for the first time 10 years ago, in 2015.

Then there's plenty of quizzes, giving you the chance to pit your Chelsea knowledge against your friends and family, and so much more besides!

By reading this Welcome message you are already well on your way to becoming a hardcore Chelsea fan. By the end of this Annual, you'll be brimming with Blues knowledge.

Enjoy!

Contents

Stamford Bridge

is fired up for the 2024/25 season, as the crowd awaits the teams ahead of our pre-season friendly with Inter Milan in August.

ENZO MARESCA

We take a look at our new head coach's story and his journey to the Bridge...

CHELSEA AMBITION

Enzo Maresca took charge of Chelsea at the start of this season and told us how he likes to coach as soon as he arrived.

"I think every manager has their own idea or style," he said. "Mine is quite clear. We are going to try to be an aggressive team on the ball and off the ball and we need to create this connection between the fans and the club, especially at home.

"One of the reasons I'm here is because I'm convinced the squad is very good and full of talent. The most important thing now is we're able to create the right culture that drives us for the season.

"I always say the same: if you are able to improve players then you are able to improve the team. So it's our target to try to improve all of them day by day."

WELL-TRAVELLED PLAYER

He is a young coach, but he has a lot of experience in the game, having played in England, Italy, Spain and Greece. An all-round midfielder, with good technique, a great work rate and an eye for the occasional goal, Maresca won trophies with Juventus and Sevilla, and learned his trade as a young player with West Bromwich Albion in the late 1990s. He also played for Italy from Under-15s through to Under-21s level.

RISING TO THE TOP

Maresca ended his playing career in 2017 and became a coach with Italian club Ascoli. Then, in 2020, he moved to England to begin working as a coach at Manchester City, where he took charge of their development squad (Under-

21s team) and led them to the Premier League 2 title. It was a sign of his ability as a coach, and he left the next season to take charge of Parma, then in the second tier of Italian football in 2021, before returning to Manchester City as part of Pep Guardiola's first-team coaching staff a year later. It was in Maresca's year working with them that they won the Treble for the first time, adding further to his reputation as a young coach with huge potential.

WINNING HABIT

Leicester City hired Maresca in the summer of 2023 to take them back to the Premier League following their relegation the previous season. He brought the team together, built a clear style of play and won the Championship with 97 points, earning him the chance to coach Chelsea this season.

When he took on the role at Stamford Bridge, he asked Blues fans to "trust the process, trust the idea, be behind the team." He aims to build a clear way of playing here, but he is also excited by the prospect of leading a club with a global fan base and big ambitions.

"I consider Chelsea one of the biggest clubs in the world," he said. "We are going to enjoy the journey. Like at every club, for every manager, it will not be easy because nothing is easy. But for sure we are going to enjoy our journey."

CHELSEA'S
Italian LINK

Enzo Maresca is the seventh Italian to take charge of the Chelsea men's team and he is in very good company...

■ GIANLUCA VIALLI
■ 1998-2000

The legendary Italian striker had signed for Chelsea as a player in 1996, when he had just lifted the Champions League trophy as captain of Juventus the previous season. Ruud Gullit was our manager at the time, and although he was Dutch he had achieved fame and success in Italy as a player too. He lost his job in February 1998, and Vialli took over as player-manager, guiding us to the League Cup and the European Cup Winners' Cup within months of taking over. The following year his Blues team won the UEFA Super Cup and just fell short in the Premier League title race, before he reached the quarter-finals of the Champions League and won the FA Cup in 1999/00. He left just weeks after winning the Charity Shield (as the Community Shield was then known) the following season.

■ CLAUDIO RANIERI
■ 2000-2004

Vialli's replacement was another Italian, but Ranieri was not nearly so well known. In fact, most Chelsea fans had to look up who he was! He didn't start too well, as he tried to introduce younger players to an ageing squad, but we reached the FA Cup final in 2002, losing to Arsenal. Then, in his third season, he steered us to fourth place despite having no money to spend at all. That changed when Roman Abramovich became owner in the summer of 2003, and we got to the semi-finals of the Champions League and finished second under Ranieri in 2003/04, but he was replaced by Jose Mourinho that summer, without having won a trophy at Chelsea. He later became world famous when he won the Premier League with Leicester City in 2015/16.

CARLO ANCELOTTI
2009-2011

Ancelotti has made plenty of headlines recently for winning trophies with Real Madrid, and he also brought his magic touch to Stamford Bridge when he took over 15 years ago. He had already been a great success at AC Milan when he arrived in London, and he led Chelsea to the first League and FA Cup Double in our history in 2009/10. We scored more than 100 goals in the Premier League alone that season, with a front three of Didier Drogba, Nicolas Anelka and Florent Malouda, not to mention supersub Salomon Kalou and midfield goal machine, Frank Lampard. After securing the league title with an 8-0 win over Wigan Athletic on the final day of the season, we then won the FA Cup by beating Portsmouth 1-0 at Wembley.

ROBERTO DI MATTEO
2012

Di Matteo had been our midfield marvel in the late 1990s, under Gullit and Vialli. He had scored goals in three Wembley cup finals and was already a Chelsea legend when he returned as assistant manager to Andre Villas-Boas in 2011. However, the Italian added a new chapter to his Blues story when he took over as manager after Villas-Boas lost his job in early 2012. Di Matteo led us to another FA Cup success at the end of the domestic season, then achieved something that no Chelsea manager had previously done – he won the Champions League, as we beat Bayern Munich on penalties in the final at the German club's own stadium.

ANTONIO CONTE
2016-2018

Conte had been head coach of the Italy national team before he took over at Chelsea in the summer of 2016. The Italy team are nicknamed the 'Azzurri', which is Italian for 'Blues', so he was used to the nickname already! He took over a Chelsea team that had finished in mid-table the previous season and led us to the Premier League title thanks to a 3-4-3 formation that shook up English football. Conte had the chance to match Ancelotti's achievement when we made it to the FA Cup final in 2017 too, but we fell at the final hurdle, losing to Arsenal. The next season, we weren't so special in the league, finishing fifth, but we did win the FA Cup, beating Manchester United 1-0 in the Wembley final, which was Conte's last game in charge.

MAURIZIO SARRI
2018-2019

We once again turned to Italy for Conte's replacement, choosing a coach who hadn't been a professional player. Sarri had become a hero with his style of play at Napoli and he hoped to achieve the same with Chelsea. He had never won a trophy in elite football before and this was his best chance yet, so he set to work teaching the squad his patient 4-3-3 system. It took some time for us to get going and there were times when it looked like we might struggle, but we reached the League Cup final and were unstoppable in the Europa League that season. We went all the way to the final in UEFA's second competition and beat Arsenal 4-1 in a London derby final played almost 3,000 miles away in Baku, capital of Azerbaijan! Finally, Sarri got his hands on silverware, before leaving Stamford Bridge after one season in the dugout.

MEET THE *New* BOYS!

There were some new arrivals at Chelsea over the summer. Let's get to know them...

PEDRO NETO

The Portuguese winger joined us from Wolves a week before the start of the season, on a seven-year contract. The 24-year-old burst onto the scene as a teenage talent with his first club, Braga, before achieving success during a two-year spell with Italian club Lazio, where he won the Italian Cup in 2018/19. Since then, he has spent five years in the Premier League, during which he was one of Wolves' most dangerous players and became a Portugal international.

TOSIN ADARABIOYO

Tosin joined us on a free transfer from our west London neighbours Fulham ahead of pre-season. The centre-back signed a four-year deal with Chelsea and started his career at Manchester City, where he made his debut against Chelsea at Stamford Bridge as a teenager in an FA Cup tie back in February 2016. He has since made over 200 professional appearances and said he was coming 'full circle' when he joined because he was born just down the road from Stamford Bridge, at St Mary's Hospital, in Paddington.

KIERNAN DEWSBURY-HALL

Dewsbury-Hall linked up with his former Leicester boss Enzo Maresca when he agreed a five-year contract at Chelsea in the summer. The midfielder played for the Foxes almost 200 times and was their supporters' and players' Player of the Year last season as they won the Championship. His 12 goals and 14 assists saw him included in the league's Team of the Season. A huge fan of darts and snooker, he is good friends with four-time world snooker champion, Mark Selby.

FILIP JORGENSEN

The young goalkeeper signed from Villarreal during pre-season, having made 37 appearances for the Spanish club last season and made the most saves in La Liga during the 2023/24 campaign. Born in Sweden, he represents Denmark Under-21s at international level, having a Danish father and a Swedish mother. The 6ft 3in keeper joined Villarreal's youth setup in 2017, having previously been on the books at Real Mallorca and Malmo, among other clubs, as a youngster. He made his first-team debut in December 2021, at the age of 19.

OMARI KELLYMAN

Kellyman is a teenage attacking midfielder who signed from Aston Villa on a six-year deal in the summer. The England Under-19s international started out in the Derby County academy before moving across the Midlands to join Villa two years ago. He made his professional debut last season in a UEFA Conference League game against Hibernian and went on to make his Premier League bow against Manchester City in April 2024.

RENATO VEIGA

This Portugal Under-21s international can play in both defence and midfield, and joined us from Swiss club Basel on a seven-year contract with a further one-year option. The son of former Cape Verde international footballer Nelson Veiga, Renato started out in the academy of Portuguese giants Sporting Lisbon, before moving on loan to German Bundesliga club Augsburg in January 2023. His performances earned him a move to Basel, where he made 26 appearances in all competitions in the 2023/24 season.

MARC GUIU

Spanish striker Guiu joined Chelsea on a five-year deal from Barcelona just before pre-season got started. He made headlines in Spain when he scored a winning goal with his second touch in professional football, finding the net 23 seconds after coming off the bench for his senior debut against Athletic Bilbao in October 2023. The Spain Under-19s international was just 17 years and 291 days at the time, and became the club's fastest and youngest debutant goalscorer.

NOAH KAHAN
x *Chelsea*

The American singer-songwriter has taken the music world by storm in recent years, with his chart-topping album 'Stick Season' streamed billions of times and fans across the planet packing out venues wherever he goes. But few things in life give him as much pleasure as Chelsea Football Club, as he explains to us...

Why Chelsea?

So, my neighbours in Strafford, Vermont, lived part-time in London and, I believe, next to Frank Lampard for a certain amount of time! I didn't really have a team that was mine for a sport that I loved playing growing up, and my neighbours would come back from London talking about Frank Lampard and wearing Chelsea jerseys, always using Chelsea in FIFA, and it kind of became a really interesting thing for me. I really fell in love with that 2009/10 team under Carlo Ancelotti – like, deeply in love! I had the jersey, I watched every game, and I kind of just became obsessed really quickly. My mum and I would watch every single game together. If friends stayed over, they knew they were getting up at 7am to watch Chelsea! When we had Champions League games, my mum would drive up to the school and take me out – I'd skip my last class to watch Chelsea! It just became this thing that was part of our relationship together, something we could support, and it's carried on into adulthood for me. For better and for worse!

Mostly good though, right?!

Yeah, mostly better. Since I started watching, we've had so much success. I obviously wasn't around in periods of less trophies, I came in and we were really winning a lot, and I got so used to it that sometimes it's hard when you don't win. But remember, that's just part of being a fan. Supporting in victory and defeat.

What's it like following from afar?
From a timezone perspective, especially on tour, it's hard. We were in Australia and waking up at 3.45am to watch Chelsea play. It's a commitment! I love it man, it's a real passion and, for me, it's an escape from stress. I live with a lot of stress on the road, in my career and in my life, and Chelsea has always been this other thing. Sure, sometimes it stresses me out too, but it's a place where I can go to be somebody else. When I watch Chelsea, I'm just one of millions of Chelsea supporters, instead of a musician on tour.

Who's your all-time favourite player?
Didier Drogba. Everything he represented as a player and a person, for the team. But I could pick so many players here that I've loved watching. I had a John Mikel Obi jersey at one time! Fernando Torres, N'Golo Kante, Frank Lampard, Florent Malouda, Juan Mata, Petr Cech... I could keep naming them. My mum always loved Branislav Ivanovic because she thought he had a nice butt, so I'll put him in for that!

Which player would you pick, past or present, to guest with you on a song?
That's easy: Petr Cech! He's a world-class drummer, he can come and play drums for us. He's truly a Renaissance man! He's also played as a hockey goaltender. Being a drummer, it takes so much intelligence and rhythm, and understanding of tempo and music and art.

You played football as a kid. Who would you compare yourself to?
I was a striker and I'm trying to think of a comparison I can make, but there's no player as slow as me! I was born with a footballing mind, but not the body.

Maybe Olivier Giroud is a decent comparison. You never looked at him trying to get down the line and boost past the defender, but he was always in the right place and that's where I feel like I thrived – being in the right place, seeing the right pass and making the right runs.

If you could go back in time, would you rather have become a famous singer or a professional footballer?
I'd probably be a singer because there's so much unpredictability with the health of football players, especially the workload now at the top level. Football is also very results based and binary. In music you find a niche... some people admire guitar playing, or songwriters, or a great voice, but you don't necessarily need to have all three, but in football you've got to be the best. So, I'd probably still be a singer, but I'd do anything to suit up for Chelsea on a Champions League night. I would give it all away, for sure. The moment Chelsea won

the Champions League is as happy as I've ever been with anything in music, I was just as excited. So, they're pretty even.

What do you love most about being a Chelsea fan?
I think it's almost become so ingrained in my own life that, of course I love Chelsea and I love watching the games, but for me it's feeling like a kid again. Waking up, turning on the TV, looking at the team sheet, being excited, being frustrated, rooting for a player that's got a chance to start... just being able to escape the world for 90 minutes of pure joy. Chelsea has always been an escape for me. What I love the most is probably the memories I have associated with it. How it's brought me closer to my mum and to this culture of football, which is really beautiful. It's brought me so much joy over the years, and I'm grateful for every second of being a Chelsea fan.

Noah's top three CFC moments

1 Didier Drogba's header in the 2012 Champions League final. You knew that Chelsea team wasn't done. We were getting dominated by an amazing Bayern team, but you just had that feeling that we were going to win, no matter what. As Gary Neville said, it was written in the stars. Watching Drogba score that header was just a validation of magic for me.

2 Second favourite, very 2012 heavy, is Fernando Torres' goal against Barcelona in the semi-final. I really relate to the struggling striker, the low confidence striker. At the end, Torres just breaks and it's the culmination of all the hope I had for this guy

taking place in a 10-second span. When he scored, you could just see it on his face, his cheeks flushed red, he was so happy. I was so happy for him. It was at a time in my life when I really needed something good. It was just a crazy moment of emotion.

3 There's so many more I could pick, but it's got to be another Champions League one: Kai Havertz's goal against Manchester City to win it in 2021. Looking back, having it be during Covid was a little harder because there was so much going on in the world, but that Havertz goal just provided a moment of magic, and it won us the Champions League.

BACK-TO-BACK-TO-BACK -TO-BACK-TO-BACK

Chelsea Women have long been the dominant force in the Women's Super League, with last season's title the fifth (yes, fifth!) in a row to be won by the Blues. Here's a reminder of how that triumph was secured, along with a look back at the four that preceded it...

When Millie Bright and Emma Hayes raised the WSL trophy for the seventh time together, following a thumping 6–0 victory over Manchester United at Old Trafford, both the captain and our outgoing manager expressed the same sentiment: this had been the toughest one yet.

At one point, despite Hayes' announcement early in the season that she would be ending her long tenure at the helm, it looked like we'd be heading for a fifth straight title at

a canter. Then, as the campaign neared its conclusion, the trophy appeared to have slipped from our grasp and into the hands of Manchester City.

But when all was said and done, and the final whistle had been blown on the 2023/24 season, there was that familiar sight of an era-defining group of players lifting yet more silverware, creating memories that will last for a lifetime. This is how they did it...

After kicking off the season with a win at Stamford Bridge, Guro Reiten's late equaliser against Manchester City on matchweek two gave us an early indication of the thrills and spills to come over the next nine months.

A fabulous hat-trick from Sjoeke Nusken against Brighton was some way for the Germany international to announce herself to Blues fans, and as the season progressed her goals would play a huge part in our success.

The ever-dependable Sophie Ingle made history against Liverpool when she set a new record for the most appearances in the history of the WSL, although it wasn't just the old guard doing the business. Academy graduate Aggie Beever-Jones was on target at the Bridge too as she enjoyed a breakthrough campaign.

But the star of the show against the Reds was Lauren James, who scored a hat-trick at the Bridge – which she followed up with another treble at our SW6 home against Manchester United at the start of 2024. With Sam Kerr suffering a season-ending injury, LJ really stepped up to the plate.

Catarina Macario had to wait a long time to make her Chelsea debut after joining the club. But more than 600 days on from her last competitive game, she needed only six minutes to get off the mark as a Blue!

We played four WSL games at Stamford Bridge in 2023/24, the last of which was against Arsenal. Backed by a huge crowd, the Blues thumped the Gunners thanks to the brilliance of James and Nusken.

Although we missed out on a place in the Champions League final with a narrow defeat at home to Barcelona in front of a full house at the Bridge, the title race was back in our hands when we capitalised on a Manchester City defeat to thump Bristol City 8-0 in Hayes' last home game as Chelsea boss.

Going into the final day, we led the league on goal difference – and six more goals against Manchester United at Old Trafford, taking us to an all-time WSL best of 71 for the season, ensured that the trophy would be staying at Kingsmeadow for another year.

BACK-TO-BACK-TO-BACK-TO-BACK-TO-BACK

2019/20

The Blues' third WSL title, and first of this run of five, was unlike any other in the history of English football! The coronavirus pandemic meant no fixtures took place after we'd beaten Arsenal to win the Continental League Cup final at the end of February. For the first time ever, the WSL standings were decided on a points-per-game basis – and we'd just done enough to edge out Manchester City and Arsenal, our nearest rivals against whom we took 10 points out of 12, to secure the title.

The campaign had started with a bang in front of 25,000 supporters at Stamford Bridge, when Bethany England scored a stunner to set the tone for an incredible season for both her and the club. She finished as our top scorer and was named Player of the Year as we swept aside the competition, and she netted a vital goal in our 3-3 draw against Manchester City in what proved to be our last league fixture of the shortened season. That result ultimately meant we finished just ahead of City when the standings were finalised.

Unlike the glorious celebrations that follow most trophies, on this occasion the squad were informed of their triumph during a team meeting over Zoom!

2020/21

Although this campaign is probably best remembered for our thrilling run to a first-ever Champions League final, albeit one which ended in defeat to Barcelona, it was a historic league campaign as we retained the title for the first time in our history. On top of that, we also won the Community Shield, kept hold of the Conti Cup and later added the FA Cup to complete the Quadruple!

With Sam Kerr, who had signed at the start of 2020, and Pernille Harder, a record signing for women's football following her move from Wolfsburg, in our ranks, we were simply unstoppable in the domestic game. In fact, our form was so good that we set a new record for the longest unbeaten run in WSL history, going 33 matches without defeat before a surprise loss at home to Brighton in February.

Kerr and Fran Kirby, dubbed 'Kerr-by' by the supporters, formed a formidable strike pairing to fire us to glory, with the former winning the WSL Golden Boot and Kirby becoming the club's leading scorer in the modern era.

The title celebrations were once again not quite what you'd expect as, with Covid-19 still preventing crowds at football matches, we celebrated at an empty Kingsmeadow – with the supporters cheering from outside the ground!

2021/22

Our third straight WSL title was won in thrilling fashion on the final day, at the end of a campaign in which we won two FA Cup finals against our biggest rivals. That's right, two FA Cup finals in one season!

Normality was starting to return as the fans were back in the stadium, just in time to see Emma Hayes take charge of her 250th game as Chelsea Women manager and for Fran Kirby to become the first player to hit a century of goals for the club since the start of the WSL in 2011.

An FA Cup final triumph over Arsenal in December, once again due to Covid-19 enforced delays, was a big boost to our league campaign, which required us to be almost perfect between January and mid-May.

Twelve straight wins in all competitions secured another FA Cup, this time with victory over Manchester City, and the WSL – although we did it the hard way against Manchester United on the final day. Twice trailing to the Red Devils, Sam Kerr's spectacular brace ensured our name remained on the trophy for another year...

2022/23

One thing that was said time and time again about Chelsea Women during this remarkable run of success is that the players always seemed to find a way to win. This season typified that mentality and, having held off Manchester City and Arsenal in previous campaigns, on this occasion it was Manchester United who fell at the hands of this winning machine.

An opening-day defeat to Liverpool meant we spent almost the whole season playing catch-up, although it was one of only two losses we suffered in the league all year – and the second wasn't until the spring. Either side of those results we went on epic winning runs, the type of which we came to expect on a yearly basis from the Blues.

Man United were beaten home and away, Arsenal were vanquished at Kingsmeadow on the penultimate weekend of the season, and all that was left was for Guro Reiten, one of our standout attacking players all season, and Co to help put the seal on yet another title triumph on the final day at Reading.

Throw in an FA Cup final win over Manchester United that was settled by Sam Kerr – who else? – and it was another remarkable chapter in our history.

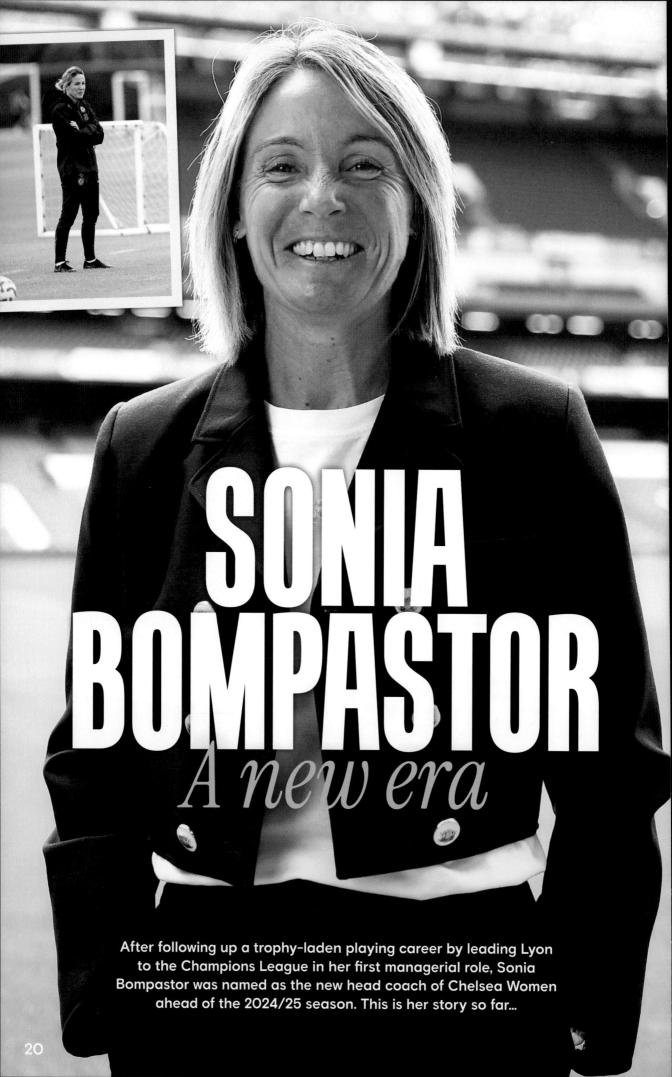

SONIA BOMPASTOR
A new era

After following up a trophy-laden playing career by leading Lyon to the Champions League in her first managerial role, Sonia Bompastor was named as the new head coach of Chelsea Women ahead of the 2024/25 season. This is her story so far...

MAGIC ON THE PITCH

"What a brilliant player. An unbelievable left-back with a wand of a left foot." Those were the words of Emma Hayes, Bompastor's predecessor in the Chelsea Women dugout, to describe her as a player after the pair worked together at Washington Freedom, where Hayes was on the coaching staff.

She wasn't alone in having a high opinion of Bompastor during her playing days, which were filled with trophies and a long stint in the France national team.

As well as her two-season spell in the USA, Bompastor won trophies galore with Montpellier and Lyon in her homeland. Overall, she won the French league eight times, the Coupe de France four times and, most famously, two Champions Leagues while at Lyon. She was also chosen as the best female footballer in France on two occasions.

Although major silverware eluded her at international level, she scored 19 times in 156 appearances for her country across a 12-year stint in the national team.

LEARNING HER TRADE

Bompastor maintained her link with Lyon after hanging up her boots in 2013, shortly after captaining the club in a Champions League final defeat at Stamford Bridge in one of her final appearances as a professional footballer.

She took up a coaching position at the club's academy, where she helped bring through the next generation of talent over the course of eight years. Plenty of those who came through under Bompastor went on to help the senior side to Champions League glory as Lyon dominated the European game.

Then, in the final weeks of the 2020/21 campaign, Lyon parted company with their head coach and the

decision was taken to promote from within – and they turned to Bompastor.

EUROPEAN GLORY

Before Bompastor took charge of the first team, Lyon had suffered a Champions League quarter-final exit to fierce rivals Paris Saint-Germain. Her first task was as simple as it was daunting – bring back the trophy.

Their run in continental competition that year wasn't without its challenges, but they overcame holders Barcelona in a thrilling final in Turin, scoring three times in the first half – including one for Cat Macario – to secure a famous victory.

Having lifted the trophy twice as a player, Bompastor had once again climbed the summit of the women's game. She became the first female to win the Champions League as both a player and a head coach.

It was one of seven trophies she won during her time in charge at Lyon over the course of three years at the helm.

TRUSTED COACHES

It's not just Bompastor who joined us in the summer from Lyon. She was also accompanied by her trusted assistants, Camille Abily and Theo Rivrin.

Abily spent five years as assistant coach at Lyon, working with Bompastor and her predecessor Jean-Luc Vasseur. Like Bompastor, Abily made the move into coaching after enjoying a successful playing career of her own.

She won numerous trophies in France with Lyon and Montpellier – where she was a team-mate of Bompastor – including five Champions Leagues, and also played in the United States in two spells with Los Angeles Sol and FC Gold Pride. She also won more than 180 caps for France before hanging up her boots in 2018.

Rivrin, meanwhile, worked as Bompastor's assistant at Lyon and was previously the head coach of their Under-19s team.

Aiming for the top

From the moment she set foot into Chelsea Football Club, Bompastor made it clear that her expectations are perfectly aligned with her new employers. And that means aiming right for the top.

"Chelsea is one of the best clubs in Europe. When you come here, you can just feel the ambitions of the club. This is the place where most of the coaches want to be – and I was the one who had the chance!

"I've had the opportunity and the chance to win the Champions League as a coach and as a player, and I really want to make sure I give my best here to win the Champions League with another club in another country.

"I like when I have high expectations; I like this pressure. Chelsea is a club that already won a lot of titles. They are the best club in England. I will be happy if everyone is expecting Chelsea to win the Champions League because this is why we came. I know the players and all the staff are going to work to make sure we achieve this goal."

BRONZE
is a
BLUE

Lucy Bronze is one of the most decorated players in the history of English football, and she's set her sights on adding to her impressive medal collection with Chelsea

THE NEXT CHAPTER

"To be at a club like Chelsea that is renowned for winning trophies, it's a perfect match-up. I know people always say that I've won so many trophies, and I've won the Champions League so many times, but I've never won the Champions League with an English team in my career. Don't get me wrong, being English and playing abroad were fantastic experiences and I wouldn't change it for anything. But I've never done that with an English club and want to achieve this."

MADE IN AMERICA

"I went to America to play football when I was 17 and it had a huge influence on me. It was where I realised being so competitive was *it*. Not only was it okay, but it was the right way to be competitive, to want to win. I think the US have always had that strong mentality that we've not seen as much in Europe. I went there and I was like a kid in a candy shop. They're so determined. Their mentalities are crazy. That's what I wanted to be. I've realised since that winning is addictive – that comes from my time in the US and how competitive it was."

BRIGHT BUDDY

"Where do I start with Millie? She is the player that I've played with the longest who's here at Chelsea. I think the thing that Millie and I best get on with is when we're in games. We know each other's games inside out. With her physicality, I always know she is going to be strong next to me. I trust her 100 per cent. We're both leaders in the teams we've been in – and not only do we want to win but we want to push other players and help them realise their potential. We're often thinking the same thing about pushing everyone and making sure our standards are high."

FAMILIAR FACES

"I know both Sonia [Bompastor] and Camille [Abily, assistant coach] really well from my time at Lyon. It's a new era at Chelsea as well, that I want to be part of. Emma [Hayes] obviously was amazing for this club and took it to a high level. But those two are another big reason for wanting to come here. I played with Camille in my first season, she was then a coach as well. She is someone I learnt a lot from and she had a big influence in an important part of my career. I've always kept in touch with her. She's a friend even though she's my coach now. The type of players both of them were… there's not many in the game who are better to learn from."

ROARING LIONESS

"Scoring against Norway at the 2015 World Cup was a pivotal moment where I really realised that, for me personally, I had an opportunity to go and be one of the best players in the game, to push myself. I just think it changed the way I saw myself, and the way women's football was viewed changed a little bit after that tournament. Not just because of me, but because of the whole team and achieving something with England by reaching the semi-finals. It was a moment that led to so much more, obviously like winning the Euros and making the World Cup final."

PLENTY MORE TO COME

"I absolutely love football. It's what I would have done whether I became a professional or not. And anyone who knows me will say I'm the most competitive person. Playing football at the highest level, I want to do it for as long as possible, winning trophies for as long as possible. I'm motivated and driven to do that. I always have been, and I think always will be. I'm sure eventually someone will have to drag me off the pitch rather than me saying, 'No I don't want to play.'"

NEW ERA

The summer of 2024 also brought with it a number of other new faces who are here to write the next chapter in the illustrious history of Chelsea Women

SANDY BALTIMORE

After nine years and more than 200 appearances, Baltimore said goodbye to Paris Saint-Germain to take the next step in her career as a Blue, bringing both international and Champions League experience to the table. Predominantly a wide player, she is naturally left-footed but comfortable playing on either flank or in central attacking roles, thanks to her excellent technical ability.

FRIENDS REUNITED

"I have known Eve Perisset for a very long time, we played together at PSG and we see each other a lot with the national team. She told me that if I come to Chelsea then I am definitely going to love it! I also played with Ashley Lawrence in Paris. It is important for me to have those relationships when coming to a new club. Knowing them gives me more confidence for when I am playing. It will help me feel a bit freer to focus on the football."

NEXT STEP

"I started playing at Paris Saint-Germain at a very young age, and the fact I started playing there so young means I have grown up with football and I had to mature quite fast. I'm hoping I can keep growing and continue that development here at Chelsea. I want to be able to bring the technical qualities that I have and use them to help the team. I hope the fans will be able to see my technical abilities and my ability to move the ball around to my team-mates. At Chelsea, I want to improve tactically and the physical side of my game."

JULIA BARTEL

One of the top young players in Europe, Bartel joined us from Barcelona, where she came up through the ranks of the reigning Champions League holders after moving to them as a 15-year-old. Her technical ability and tactical intelligence came to the fore during her appearances for Barca's B side and she's also regularly captained both club and country at youth level, winning the Under-20 World Cup with Spain.

HERE TO WIN

"I am a very ambitious person, so I'm all about winning, winning, winning. I think I'll fit in at Chelsea, as I know what is expected from a player who plays for this club. My short-term goal is to learn here, keep improving and make the most of being surrounded by amazing players. My long-term goal is to win everything I can possibly win here at Chelsea."

BON IDOL

"I'm very grateful for my time with Barcelona and every moment in the academy. They pay a lot of attention to minor details and are able to really develop players. I'm also very grateful that I could spend so much time in Barcelona training with Aitana Bonmati from Barcelona, learning certain things from her, as she is my idol in football. Aitana would be the player who has influenced me the most so far."

ORIANE JEAN-FRANCOIS

Another summer arrival from Paris Saint-Germain, Jean-Francois brings dynamism and versatility to the Chelsea midfield as a player who is comfortable in the holding role or playing as a more traditional box-to-box midfielder. She debuted for Paris FC just before her 18th birthday and made her first senior international appearance a year later, before moving across the city to PSG.

BLUE IDOLS

"I know a lot about Chelsea because I come from French Guiana and Florent Malouda [former men's team winger] also comes from there. Because of him, I supported Chelsea when I was younger. But my role model is N'Golo Kante. He is humble and he plays for the team. For him, the most important thing is the team before himself and that is how I like to think on the pitch, too."

KEEPING COOL

"When I was younger I did taekwondo. It helped me to be calm on the pitch. It is important because the first thing with football is that it is a game. I really love football, it is my passion, so I want to have fun when I play. That is most important to me. If I am calm then it helps me play and helps the team play. If we are thinking and worrying about the result before playing the game then I won't be playing well."

23

Chelsea CONNECTIONS QUIZ

1 Which former Chelsea goalkeeper (pictured) returned as assistant first-team coach this season?

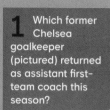

3 Which Chelsea player was part of that Championship-winning team under Maresca last season, before moving to Stamford Bridge in the summer?

2 Which current Premier League club did Enzo Maresca coach to the Championship title last season?

4 At which Premier League club were Romeo Lavia and Cole Palmer team-mates as youngsters?

5 Benoit Badiashile and which other Chelsea player were defensive partners at Monaco before they moved to England?

6 Robert Sanchez, Marc Cucurella, Moises Caicedo and Levi Colwill all played for which other Premier League club before Chelsea?

7 Catarina Macario has been reunited with her former coach, Sonia Bompastor, at Chelsea this season. But which French club did they win the Women's Champions League with in 2021/22?

8 Three other Chelsea Women players have also won the Champions League with the same French club. Name any of them for a point.

9 How many of the current Chelsea Women squad were part of the England Lionesses squad that won Euro 2022?

☐ A: 2

☐ B: 3

☐ C: 4

10 Zecira Musovic, Nathalie Bjorn and Johanna Rytting Kaneryd all play together for which national team?

MEN'S PLAYER OF THE SEASON 2023/24
Cole Palmer

Cole Palmer's first season at Chelsea was nothing short of sensational. He was at the heart of our attacking play, his skills were breathtaking and he ended up winning enough awards to fill a shelf in one year. Let's take a look at what makes Palmer such a special talent...

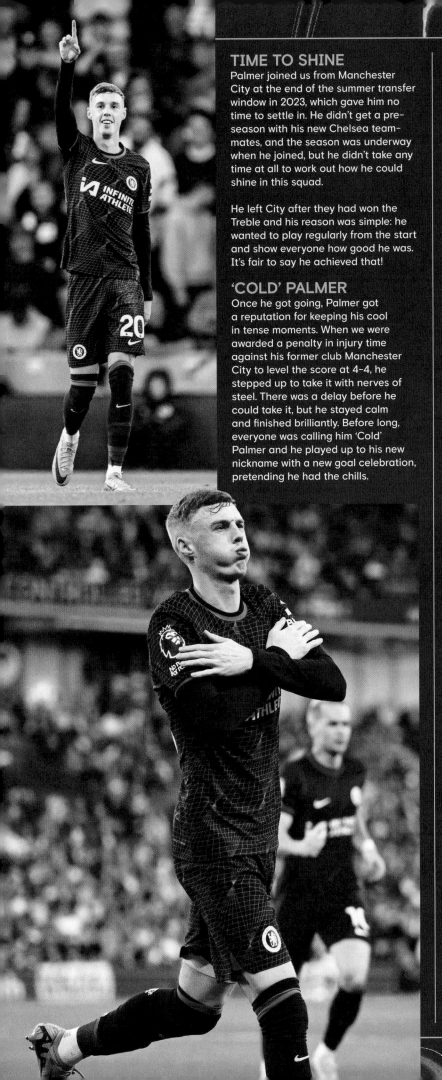

TIME TO SHINE

Palmer joined us from Manchester City at the end of the summer transfer window in 2023, which gave him no time to settle in. He didn't get a pre-season with his new Chelsea team-mates, and the season was underway when he joined, but he didn't take any time at all to work out how he could shine in this squad.

He left City after they had won the Treble and his reason was simple: he wanted to play regularly from the start and show everyone how good he was. It's fair to say he achieved that!

'COLD' PALMER

Once he got going, Palmer got a reputation for keeping his cool in tense moments. When we were awarded a penalty in injury time against his former club Manchester City to level the score at 4-4, he stepped up to take it with nerves of steel. There was a delay before he could take it, but he stayed calm and finished brilliantly. Before long, everyone was calling him 'Cold' Palmer and he played up to his new nickname with a new goal celebration, pretending he had the chills.

GOAL MACHINE

Palmer was involved in 33 Premier League goals in his first season with Chelsea, scoring 22 and assisting 11. In all competitions, his goals tally was 25... and he isn't even an out-and-out striker, usually playing behind the frontman in an attacking midfield role. He has proven himself to be that rare thing – a creator and a finisher.

His team-mate and friend, Noni Madueke, said it best: "Cole's a unique talent. He doesn't look like much of an athlete to the eye, but he's got a wiry quickness and really clean movements. His left foot is a wand... he's one of my favourite players, to be honest."

"THE BEST MONTHS OF MY CAREER"

Palmer's influence last season was made clear when awards season came around. He ended the season as Chelsea's Men's Player of the Season and our Men's Players' Player of the Season, meaning the fans and his team-mates voted him our best performer. He was awarded the PFA Fans' Player of the Year, and also won the Premier League's Young Player of the Season and Game Changer of the Season award for inspiring our 4-3 win over Manchester United in April 2024 with a dramatic hat-trick. So, how did the man himself sum up that first season in Chelsea blue?

"They've been some amazing months, to be fair, probably the best months of my career. I've been playing a lot of football and playing well, and it's been amazing. It's been about the opportunity, the platform we're trying to build, the project, and the love from the fans."

PALMER
Again!

Palmer's 33 league goal involvements in his first season here gave him a place among the Chelsea greats of the Premier League era, and made him the youngest member of an exclusive club...

THE 30+ CLUB

Only five Chelsea players have totalled more than 30 goals and assists in a Premier League season, and Cole Palmer joined that club last season. He became the first Blues player under the age of 21 to do so, and the first new signing to reach that total in his first season here since Jimmy Floyd Hasselbaink in 2000/01.

Frank Lampard is the only Chelsea player to have managed more than 30 Premier League goal involvements in a season twice, and the other two to have done so are Eden Hazard and Didier Drogba, who holds the record with 39 goals and assists in 2009/10.

	Player	Season	Goals	Assists	Total
	Didier Drogba	2009/2010	29	10	39
	Frank Lampard	2009/2010	22	14	36
	Cole Palmer	2023/2024	22	11	33
	Jimmy Floyd Hasselbaink	2000/2001	23	9	32
	Frank Lampard	2004/2005	13	18	31
	Eden Hazard	2018/2019	16	15	31

COLE'S CONTRIBUTION

A look at Palmer's stats show him to be the ultimate all-rounder.

His 22 goals made him the second-highest scorer in the Premier League last season, behind only Manchester City striker Erling Haaland, who managed 27. Nine of Palmer's goals were penalties, which was the highest number of spot kicks converted in the Premier League last season.

His 11 assists were also the second-most in the league, behind Aston Villa centre-forward Ollie Watkins, who totalled 13. Palmer was also in the top five in the league for through balls played over the course of the 2023/24 campaign, with 27. Arsenal's Martin Odegaard topped that particular table, with 39 through balls.

HOME RUN

In a period between March and April 2024, Palmer scored 11 goals in the space of five home games, including a hat-trick in our 4-3 win over Manchester United and four in our 6-0 thrashing of Everton.

By this point he was regularly leaving the crowd in disbelief with his performances, and the fans were leaving Stamford Bridge chanting: "Palmer again, ole ole!"

One goal in that memorable display against Everton stood out above all the others as he nutmegged his marker, then played a one-two with Nicolas Jackson on the edge of the box, before calmly rolling the ball inside the far post, leaving England goalie Jordan Pickford grasping air. It won the Premier League Goal of the Month award for April and was also shortlisted for Goal of the Season.

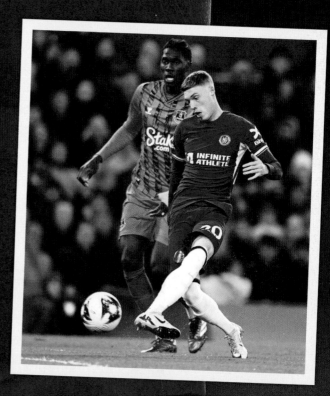

Lauren James
IS MAGIC

There's seemingly nothing Lauren James cannot do with a football at her feet –
and as our supporters sing, she's Chelsea's No10 and she scores goals with ease.
We bring you the lowdown on the reigning Chelsea Women Player of the Year

Chelsea Women have been blessed with some immensely talented footballers over the years. Two of them, Ji So-Yun and Fran Kirby, were even likened to Lionel Messi, which tells you all you need to know about just how good they were.

When you watch Lauren James in full flight, however, it quickly becomes clear that you are witnessing greatness of a different kind. The way she skips past opponents and breezes past them like they're not even there, pinging shots into the top corner from 30 yards, it's as if she's playing football down the park with her mates, instead of in front of thousands of supporters inside the stadium and sometimes millions watching at home. It takes a very special footballer to be able to do that.

Since she came to Chelsea in 2021, we've seen her improve with each passing year, but last season it was as if everything seemed to click and she went from being mentioned among the elite footballers in world football to being right at the forefront of the discussion.

We played four Women's Super League matches at Stamford Bridge in the 2023/24 season; James scored a hat-trick in two of those games, against Liverpool and Manchester United, and added two goals in the other two matches. The big stage was made for her.

And as injuries robbed us of key players at different points of the campaign, most notably the season-ending knee surgery for Sam Kerr, she was able to step up from being one of our most consistent creators to finishing as top scorer.

The sky is the limit for a player who, at 23 years of age, still has her best years ahead of her...

In her own words...

WINNING PLAYER OF THE YEAR

"It's an amazing feeling. There is loads of talent in the team and to be nominated alongside Erin Cuthbert and Jess Carter was special. It's really special to receive it. I'm really proud and hopefully I can keep developing, improving and continuing to help the team. I'm happy with what I've been able to contribute with the goals and hopefully I can continue doing that."

FREEDOM

"Anywhere on the pitch, I feel quite free. Playing as a nine is obviously different and I have to stay high and a bit more central, but I think at times I float in different positions. It's quite similar to when I'm a 10. It doesn't affect me too much because as long as I'm on the pitch, I can play my game."

ROLE REVERSAL

"It is crazy how things have changed because now it is kids coming up to me and looking at me as a role model. That was me and now they are coming up to me! I try my best to be a good role model to kids who want to play football and children in general, really, as I hope I can encourage the kids to be themselves – even with the little things like the crazy things I do with my hair! I just want kids to feel like if they want to become something, then they can do that by being themselves – just be you."

MUSIC

"My love for music has probably come from always being in changing rooms, getting ready for games. It ranges – I can go from hip-hop and rap to country. I go home and listen to music, predominantly Drake and J. Cole, Lil Durk, Lil Baby. I like Jorja Smith, I think she's a good artist."

LIFELONG LOVE

"I've always been a Chelsea supporter since a young age. I first joined the club at the age of six and I knew that even if I went away and explored different clubs, I'd end up back at Chelsea. When I came back here it was like coming home."

LEADER.
Legend.
ICON.

After a 12-year spell in charge of Chelsea Women, we said goodbye to Emma Hayes at the end of the 2023/24 season. In that time she turned the club from also-rans into the dominant force in English football, breaking down barriers along the way to change the shape of women's football forever

It seems strange to say it now, considering the level of her fame, but when Emma Hayes arrived at Chelsea in August 2012, most Blues fans were asking the same question: Who?

Although well respected within the game, thanks largely to a spell on the coaching staff at Arsenal when they won the Quadruple in 2007 and for her work in the USA, Hayes had never previously managed an English club.

She was beginning her journey with a team that had no major honours to its name and had just missed a big chance to change that fact by snatching defeat from the jaws of victory in an FA Cup final against Birmingham City. The task ahead of her, it's fair to say, was monumental.

What Hayes saw, however, was a sleeping giant ready to be awakened, with a blank canvas in front of her. Aided by Paul Green, who joined as assistant manager and soon became general manager, the football club was ready to be rebuilt, starting with the foundations.

It would take time, of course, but the club stuck with her through some difficult times early on and, gradually, improvements were made, both on and off the pitch. Player recruitment stepped up a notch, as the best players from the domestic game and abroad came in to complement the talented youngsters emerging from our Centre of Excellence.

The training facilities improved, eventually leading to Chelsea Women having their own dedicated space at our Cobham training ground, while a move to Kingsmeadow in 2017 meant the Blues had a home of their own, along with a dedicated fanbase that continues to grow with each passing year.

Then there's the trophies – lots of them. It all started with the FA Cup in 2015, secured in memorable fashion in the first-ever women's final to be played at Wembley Stadium, and there has been a steady stream of silverware ever since. Sixteen trophies, to be precise, at a time when women's football in England has never been more competitive.

They were won consistently, with very few trophy-free seasons, and in clusters – several Doubles, where league and cups were won in the same campaign, and a stunning clean sweep of all the domestic honours in the 2020/21 season.

Hayes' status at the club is, undoubtedly, legendary – but her impact has been celebrated more widely, and she was awarded an MBE in 2016, followed by an OBE in 2022. Her individual honours within the game include The Best FIFA Women's Coach for 2021.

Even in her wildest dreams, surely even she couldn't have imagined how those 12 years would have gone, not just here at Chelsea but across the women's game, worldwide. It's impossible to truly do her justice with words alone.

Thank you, Emma, for everything you have done. You're one of a kind but, more than that, you're one of us.

OVERALL RECORD

Season	Pld	W	D	L
2012	5	2	0	3
2013	18	3	2	13
2014	23	14	2	7
2015	28	20	2	6
2016	23	15	3	5
2017	11	8	2	1
2017/18	37	28	5	4
2018/19	39	26	7	6
2019/20	25	21	4	0
2020/21	40	32	4	4
2021/22	39	31	4	4
2022/23	40	32	3	5
2023/24	39	29	4	6
TOTAL	367	261	42	64

TEAM HONOURS

Women's Super League: 2015, 2017/18, 2019/20, 2020/21, 2021/22, 2022/23, 2023/24

WSL Spring Series: 2017

Women's FA Cup: 2014/15, 2017/18, 2020/21, 2021/22, 2022/23

Continental League Cup: 2019/20, 2020/21

FA Community Shield: 2020

INDIVIDUAL HONOURS

The Best FIFA Women's Coach: 2021

WSL Manager of the Season: 2015, 2017/18, 2019/20, 2020/21, 2021/22, 2022/23

LMA WSL Manager of the Season: 2017/18, 2019/20, 2020/21, 2021/22, 2022/23

Football Writers' Association Tribute award: 2024

WSL Hall of Fame: 2021

Officer of the Order of the British Empire (OBE): 2022

Member of the Order of the British Empire (MBE): 2016

FRAN-TASTIC
Memories

Chelsea Women's greatest-ever goalscorer is Fran Kirby, who left the club last summer after nine trophy-filled years as a Blue. It's safe to say Super Fran's legacy will live on for many years to come

With more than a century of goals to her name as a Chelsea Women player, Fran Kirby has set the benchmark for goalscoring in the modern era – and perhaps even more than that, with records prior to the WSL era, which started in 2011, still to be established.

However you choose to describe her 116-goal haul, one word is enough to sum up Kirby's legacy at this football club: legendary.

All but one of our 16 major honours have been won with Kirby part of the squad, with only the 2015 FA Cup secured without her. Although she joined us just prior to that triumph, following her breakthrough World Cup campaign with England, she was cup-tied for the final – but it's fair to say she made up for it over the next nine years.

She quickly established herself as one of the most renowned footballers across the globe, known for being technically gifted and clinical in front of goal, shedding the 'Mini Messi' moniker that had been placed upon her at the 2015 World Cup to become the one and only Fran Kirby.

As well as collective success, Kirby also earned numerous personal accolades at Chelsea. After scoring 25 goals in all competitions in 2017/18, she won the PFA and FWA Player of the Year awards – the first to win the female version of the latter – and the club's Women's Player and Players' Player of the Year.

Once more, her performances warranted further individual recognition in 2020/21.

She was named Chelsea Women's Player of the Year, Barclays WSL Player of the Season and PFA Players' Player of the Year – an award decided by votes of fellow professional footballers.

"Growing up, I always wanted to be the best," she said. "But the personal accolades were just a bonus on top of what we were already achieving. Everything that I've won, whether it was a team trophy, a personal trophy, a goal – it's always down to everyone else's work."

She fought back from some significant injuries and illnesses along the way and as well as becoming the first CFCW player to hit a century of goals for the club, she also became only the sixth Blue to make 200 appearances.

"I was just a young girl that loved football, and I still am that now, just a bit older! I'm just someone who loves to play football. Part of my job is to play well, win trophies and win football games, and if I'm able to do that and inspire young girls to want to be footballers, or be any form of athlete, then that's enough for me. Growing up, I never felt that I could make such an impact, so I'm really proud that I've been able to do that."

She certainly did all that and more, as well as forming a bond with the supporters that will never be broken. As she prepared to sign off from the club, her final words were reserved for those who cheered her on every step of the way.

"The club has grown so much since I first joined," she said. "From when we were playing at Staines, in front of an amazing crowd there, to selling out Stamford Bridge… it's been an incredible journey with all of you.

"Thank you for embracing me, from day one, helping me overcome some really difficult times, and sharing some amazing times with me. I will never forget how it felt to play in front of all of you, and I hope that I've left the club and the shirt in a place that means you can all be proud of me."

OH, MAREN MJELDE!

Over the course of seven years with Chelsea Women, Maren Mjelde was a manager's dream: a player who offered a consistently high level of performance in whichever position she was asked to fill, but with a propensity for providing those magic moments that most can only dream of.

Although she joined us ahead of the 2017 Spring Series as a virtual unknown on these shores, Mjelde was already a vastly experienced performer on the international stage with Norway, and we quickly found out why. Technically immaculate, tactically sound, and always up for the battle, she instantly became a fans' favourite.

Mjelde earned a spot in the PFA Team of the Year as both a defender and midfielder during her time in Blue, and she had a taste for the big occasion in the Champions League. Her late winner in a highly charged game at PSG sent us through to the semi-finals in 2019, and four years later she stepped up with a nerveless penalty with the last kick of extra time to draw us level with Lyon. Of course, she then converted the first penalty in the subsequent shoot-out as we eliminated European football's greatest-ever club side.

As her Chelsea career came to an end last season, with more than 10 major trophies lifted in that time, Mjelde perhaps summed it up best when she declared: "It's been a hell of a ride!"

HOW WELL DO YOU KNOW THE CHELSEA *Men's* FIRST TEAM?

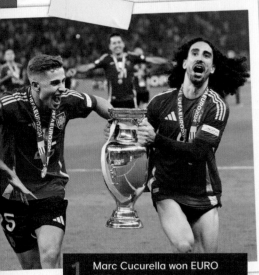

1 Marc Cucurella won EURO 2024 with Spain last summer, but which of his Chelsea team-mates scored England's goal against them in the final?

3 For which south-coast Premier League club did Romeo Lavia score against Chelsea in August 2022?

4 For which European nation did Malo Gusto make his full international debut last season?

5 Which Blues signing in the summer of 2024 played his first-ever senior match at Stamford Bridge, AGAINST Chelsea?

6 Which other summer signing was named in the UEFA Conference League Team of the Season while playing for his previous club in 2021/22?

A. Kiernan Dewsbury-Hall

B. Mykhailo Mudryk

C. Christopher Nkunku

8 Whose sensational goal from the halfway line in the final game of the 2023/24 campaign won Chelsea's Goal of the Season award?

9 It wasn't our last goal of the season, however, as we beat Bournemouth 2-1 at Stamford Bridge. Who bagged the winner that afternoon?

A. Christopher Nkunku

B. Cole Palmer

C. Raheem Sterling

10 Which Chelsea midfielder won the FIFA World Cup Young Player Award at the 2022 World Cup in Qatar?

2 Nicolas Jackson and Filip Jorgensen both joined Chelsea from the same Spanish club. Can you name the club?

7 Cole Palmer scored two hat-tricks in a month last season (including a four-goal haul against Everton), but who got Chelsea's only other hat-trick of the 2023/24 campaign?

A. Enzo Fernandez

B. Nicolas Jackson

C. Noni Madueke

Answers page 63

CHELSEA
Women's QUIZ

1 Who has played more games in the WSL than any other player in the history of the league?

- [ ] A. Millie Bright
- [ ] B. Jess Carter
- [ ] C. Sophie Ingle

2 Which player has lifted the Champions League three times with Lyon and twice with Barcelona?

- [ ] A. Lucy Bronze
- [ ] B. Kadeisha Buchanan
- [ ] C. Eve Perisset

3 Who scored two hat-tricks at Stamford Bridge in the 2023/24 season?

- [ ] A. Mia Fishel
- [ ] B. Lauren James
- [ ] C. Sam Kerr

4 Mayra Ramirez is our first-ever Colombian player, but from which Spanish club did she join us?

- [ ] A. Barcelona
- [ ] B. Levante
- [ ] C. Real Madrid

5 Which player picked up the most assists for the Blues in the 2023/24 season?

- [ ] A. Niamh Charles
- [ ] B. Lauren James
- [ ] C. Johanna Rytting Kaneryd

6 Hannah Hampton is an England international, but in which European country did she spend a large part of her childhood?

- [ ] A. Austria
- [ ] B. Spain
- [ ] C. Turkey

7 Erin Cuthbert is one of our longest-serving players. In which year did the Scottish midfielder make her debut for Chelsea?

- [ ] A. 2011
- [ ] B. 2014
- [ ] C. 2017

8 Millie Bright became Chelsea captain in the summer of 2023. Who did she replace as skipper?

- [ ] A. Karen Carney
- [ ] B. Katie Chapman
- [ ] C. Magda Eriksson

9 Sjoeke Nusken has shown herself to be a goalscoring midfielder at club level, but where has she featured most often for Germany?

- [ ] A. Centre-back
- [ ] B. Goalkeeper
- [ ] C. Striker

10 Which Scandinavian country does Nathalie Bjorn call home?

- [ ] A. Sweden
- [ ] B. Norway
- [ ] C. Denmark

FAREWELL TO A
Legend

Thiago Silva departed Chelsea at the end of last season, following four fantastic years in blue, in which time he fulfilled his destiny and finally became a Champions League winner....

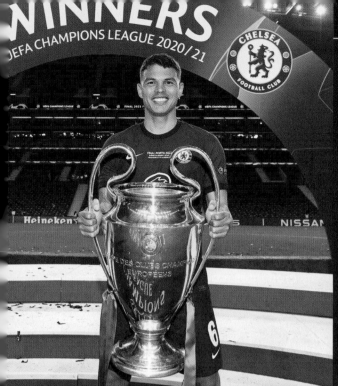

WINNERS
UEFA CHAMPIONS LEAGUE 2020/21

"HE CAME FROM PSG... TO WIN THE CHAMPIONS LEAGUE"

The Chelsea fans used to chant 'He came from PSG, to win the Champions League' in honour of Thiago Silva, the classy Brazilian centre-back who arrived here at the age of 35 having tried to win Europe's top trophy with both AC Milan and PSG. He even reached the final in 2020, in his last game for PSG, but he never gave up on his dream.

As it turned out, he achieved it in his first year with the Blues, finally getting his hands on the famous piece of silverware in Porto, where we beat Manchester City in the 2021 final. Thiago had gone off injured in the first half, but he spent the rest of the game shouting and screaming to his team-mates from the touchline.

"That was one of the hardest moments I've been through in a football match," he said. "I was playing in my second consecutive final and I wasn't able to affect the game – I was injured and on the bench. I was shouting encouragement, I was offering support as best I could because I'd been in that final before and I had an understanding of the situation. Then, when the final whistle went, it was just a huge relief."

AGE IS JUST A NUMBER

Thiago signed for Chelsea on a one-year contract in 2020, but he ended up renewing that deal three times, and remained at Stamford Bridge until he was 39 years old. In that time, he became the oldest Chelsea outfield player in our history and the oldest Chelsea goalscorer ever. When you consider that the game has become quicker and more intense with every generation, it makes that achievement even more amazing. So what was his secret to ageing so well?

"When I got to around 30 or 31, I started to think a bit differently," he said. "I got myself my own doctor and he helped me with my diet – I still have the same doctor today. So I kind of learned the hard way at a late stage of my career.

"With experience and the more time you play football, you get to a point where you start to see the game in a different light. I feel happy to be a reference or an inspiration to other people, for the youngsters that are now starting to play, and can look and see how far into their lives they could play."

FANS' FAVOURITE

At the beginning of his last game for Chelsea, Thiago was welcomed onto the pitch by the sight of a banner at each end of the pitch at Stamford Bridge, both with images of him in blue. One of them was adorned with the words to his chant, as mentioned earlier in this article, the other included the Brazil flag.

He was clearly emotional that day, and at the end of our 2-1 win over Bournemouth he was handed a microphone and spoke to the supporters, telling them he loved them. In the matchday programme that day, he tried to sum up how he felt.

"My relationship with the Chelsea supporters is hard to put into words – it was love at first sight," said Thiago. "At one point we were all fans and we know what it feels like. As a child, all I wanted to do was play football and feeling the love of the fans while you're on the pitch makes me feel very proud."

He departed Chelsea with 155 appearances and nine goals to his name. Thank you, Thiago!

BREAKTHROUGH
Blues

Last season saw another series of Chelsea Academy graduates make their debuts for the men's first-team, and two talents in particular went on to have a year to remember for the Blues...

LEVI COLWILL
Date of birth: 26.02.03
Position: Defender
Debut: 13.08.23, Liverpool (H) 1-1 D

Levi Colwill joined the Chelsea Academy at Under-9s level and made his men's first-team debut for the Blues on the opening day of last season, when he started at left-back against Liverpool at Stamford Bridge.

By that point he was already an established Premier League player, though, because he had spent the 2022/23 season on loan at Brighton & Hove Albion, where he played 22 games. Before that, he had another season-long loan, at Huddersfield Town in the Championship, giving him vital experience before he returned to play for Chelsea.

Colwill operated at centre-back and left-back last season and played 32 games in all competitions for us, but it would have been more if he hadn't missed the last two months with an injury. He scored his first

goal for the club against Brighton, the team where he had taken his first steps in the Premier League, heading in our second in a 3-2 win in December 2023.

He also made his England debut in a friendly game against Australia in October 2023, completing his rise from young prospect to full international and Chelsea first-teamer.

"I really enjoyed being in the Academy here," said Colwill about growing up here. "Chelsea's one of the best academies in the world – look at the players they've brought through – and I was just trying to become another one of the players to come through the system. I was in a great team growing up – we always made finals or won competitions – and there was kind of a family feeling from young. I think that's the best feeling you can have in football."

ALFIE GILCHRIST

Date of birth: 28.11.03
Position: Defender
Debut: 27.12.23, Crystal Palace (H) 2-1 W

Alfie Gilchrist is Chelsea through and through. His family support the Blues and his dad even created him as a player on Football Manager before he was born! Alfie says he would be in the stands at Stamford Bridge cheering on the team if he wasn't on the pitch.

He showed that passion for the badge in his men's first-team debut, when he came off the bench against Crystal Palace with only moments left to play and threw himself into two challenges immediately. The fans cheered his every move and it wasn't long before he started for the first time in our FA Cup third round win over Preston at Stamford Bridge.

Gilchrist played right-back for the men's first-team last season, but he has almost always played at centre-back in his time in the Academy, so expect to see him there at some point too. In total, he made 17 men's first-team appearances in his breakthrough season, and was named Men's Academy Player of the Year at the end of it. He also scored his first senior goal in our 6-0 win against Everton and the celebrations inside Stamford Bridge showed how much the fans have taken Alfie to their hearts.

"It's a dream come true for anyone," said Gilchrist after that goal, "but especially for me, being a fan, being here so long, coming through the Academy."

This season he has moved on loan to Sheffield United to gain more men's first-team experience with the Championship side.

The Graduates 2023/24

JOSH ASHEAMPONG
Date of birth:
05.05.06
Position: Defender
Debut: 02.05.24,
Tottenham (H)
2-0 W

MASON BURSTOW
Date of birth:
04.08.03
Position: Forward
Debut: 20.08.23,
West Ham (A)
1-3 L

LEO CASTLEDINE
Date of birth:
20.08.05
Position:
Midfielder
Debut: 23.01.24,
Middlesbrough (H)
6-1 W

MICHAEL GOLDING
Date of birth:
23.05.06
Position:
Midfielder
Debut: 06.01.24,
Preston (H) 4-0 W

ALEX MATOS
Date of birth:
03.10.04
Position:
Midfielder
Debut: 02.10.23,
Fulham (A) 2-0 W

JIMI TAURIAINEN
Date of birth:
08.03.04
Position:
Midfielder
Debut: 28.02.24,
Leeds (H) 3-2 W

PRIDE & PROGRESS

Last season was an exciting one for the Chelsea Academy, as our Under-17s and Under-18s celebrated silverware, while many players got their chance with the men's first-team...

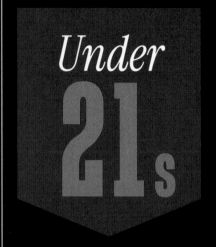

Under 21s

The Chelsea Academy is never happier than when our young players make it into the men's first-team, but there are also trophies to win and titles to chase at youth level. Last season, we were in the mix at all age levels.

The Under-21s finished fourth in the Premier League 2, which finishes with play-offs to decide the eventual winner. We beat Brighton and Arsenal to reach the semi-finals, but we lost narrowly to eventual champions Tottenham, going down 2-1. Although we always want to win the competitions we enter, Chelsea had a very young Under-21s squad last season and they came very close to going all the way under head coach Mark Robinson, who left to become

Burton Albion's men's first-team manager in the summer.

His replacement is Filipe Coelho, a highly-rated and experienced Portuguese coach who used to coach at Benfica and joined us after an impressive season as Under-23s head coach at Estoril, who topped the Portuguese Under-23s league table.

"We want to show a clear way of playing," he said at the start of the season. "We want to be dominant, but I want to see the real Chelsea way in our players. I want to see character, hunger and the players giving their all on and off the pitch."

Under 18s

The Under-18s came even closer. In fact, Hassan Sulaiman's side won the Premier League South in their age group, finishing five points clear of second-placed West Ham. That meant they qualified for the National Final against northern champions Manchester United, but they also fell to a 2-1 defeat.

"When I reflect on the season as a whole and how the players have developed, I am incredibly pleased with them all," Sulaiman said at the end of the campaign. "The boys will be disappointed with the final, but they will also be pleased with the season overall. I am looking forward to seeing a number of them progress into Under-21s football and I'm confident they will do well. I'm also confident that some of them will go on to make first-team debuts – there are a number that I know are capable of playing at that level. If they keep their heads down, keep working, focus on the areas they need to improve and build on their strengths, it is then just about timing."

Under 17s

The Under-17s isn't a regular age group in academy football. They are the first-year scholars who join the Under-18s squad after progressing from the Under-16s. However, there is one competition dedicated to their age group – the Under-17 Premier League Cup – and Chelsea are the current holders after winning it last season!

Under-18s coach Hassan Sulaiman also takes the team for these games, but his coaching staff combines with the Under-16s coaching team and last year it worked like a dream.

Chelsea's Under-17s beat Tottenham in the quarter-finals, Manchester City in the semi-finals and then overcame Wolves in the final, which was held at their ground, Molineux. The whole club was overjoyed to see our youngsters on the podium lifting the trophy after a 3-1 win.

"That team doesn't play together much – only in that tournament – and to see the way they have developed as a team over the course of the season has been fantastic," said Chelsea's former head of youth development and recruitment, Jim Fraser.

"Winning the trophy was an amazing achievement, made all the better by seeing the smiles on the faces of the players and their families. That is what it's all about, and we've got to make sure we enjoy those experiences because we want to have more of that."

Chelsea Heritage:

OUR FIRST PREMIER LEAGUE TITLE

Twenty years ago we won the Premier League for the first time, and what a team it was!

FIRST TITLE FOR 50 YEARS!

Chelsea first won the league all the way back in 1954/55, when the top flight in this country was known as the First Division. It was renamed the Premier League in 1992, and a new trophy was created for the new title.

It took until the 2004/05 season for us to finally win the new league trophy, exactly half a century since we last became champions of England, and we did it in style.

We ended the campaign with 95 points, and were 12 points clear of second-placed Arsenal. In fact, we were so dominant that year, we clinched the title with three games to go, when we won 2-0 at Bolton on 30 April. Frank Lampard scored twice that day and ended the season as our top goalscorer with 19 in all competitions, and 13 in the Premier League.

THE SPECIAL ONE

The man behind that title triumph was Jose Mourinho, who took over as Chelsea manager in the summer of 2004 after guiding Porto to Champions League glory.

He was already well-known for his confidence, but he took things to another level in his first press conference at Stamford Bridge when he told the media and the world, "I think I am a special one."

He then went and showed us all why he was special by putting together one of the strongest teams in Chelsea history, playing a solid 4-3-3 formation with the best defence in the history of the Premier League, a midfield that never stopped running and a front three that were absolutely terrifying in full flight. We won the league easily, as though it was never in doubt, and we added the League Cup for good measure, beating Liverpool 3-1 in the final.

JT AND LAMPS

The spine of the team was crucial that year, and two Londoners were at the heart of everything. Centre-back John Terry – known as 'JT' – was the skipper, and Frank Lampard was the vice-captain and midfield marvel, wearing the No8 shirt and racing from box to box to arrive just in time to score plenty of goals.

Both men were selected in the PFA Team of the Year and JT was named PFA Player of the Year, chosen by his fellow players, while Lamps won the Premier League Player of the Season and the FWA Footballer of the Year, chosen by the football media.

With world-class anchor man Claude Makelele operating as the link man between them in defensive midfield and the towering presence of Didier Drogba up front, it was the ultimate spine for a title-winning team.

DEFENCE IS KEY

We conceded a grand total of 15 goals in the 2004/05 season, which is the least of any team in Premier League history. It was legendary goalkeeper Petr Cech's first season at Chelsea, and he had the likes of Paulo Ferreira, William Gallas, Ricardo Carvalho and our captain, leader, legend, John Terry in front of him. Now, that was a solid backline – with Wayne Bridge as another option at left-back when we had a player missing.

It was all about momentum at the back for us that year, as we only conceded two goals in the first 10 games of the Premier League season, and only two opponents managed to score more than once against us all season. Cech's 24 clean sheets that season remains a league record.

WING WIZARDS

It wasn't just about controlling the centre of the pitch, though. We had wingers to scare the life out of opposition defenders. Arjen Robben was fast as lightning, Joe Cole was full of tricks and turns, and Damien Duff could run all day, not to mention his perfect eye for a well-timed run in behind the defence.

With two of those three playing out wide, Drogba and Eidur Gudjohnsen had all the supply they needed to cause havoc. It was very close to the complete team and some Chelsea fans would argue it was our strongest side ever.

2015 WSL TITLE RECAP

This year marks the 10th anniversary of Chelsea Women's first Women's Super League title. We look back at a monumental year that kickstarted an era of unprecedented success for the Blues

When 2015 began, Chelsea Women had come a long way in a short space of time – from finishing second from bottom two years earlier, to missing out on the title by the barest of margins in the very next campaign.

After Emma Hayes had taken over as manager in the summer of 2012, she had stated her ambition for her team to join "the illustrious winners at this football club at first team and youth level" – and that meant lifting silverware, something which had never been done by Chelsea at the highest level of women's football.

That goal was accomplished during a season in which we secured a sensational Double, following up an unforgettable triumph over Notts County in the first Women's FA Cup final held at Wembley Stadium by winning the WSL title. Fittingly, the league was won on the last day of the 2015 season in emphatic fashion, exactly 23 years on from the club's first-ever match, as the Blues beat Sunderland 4-0 at Wheatsheaf Park to become champions of England.

If it all sounds rather straightforward, the reality was anything but. A year earlier, Hayes and her squad were on the receiving end of a final-day defeat which yanked the WSL trophy from our grasp when we were clear favourites. The bottle of the squad was being tested to the extreme, and the manager knew it.

"If you do it once then it's a mistake, but if you do it twice then it's a choice – and that's the motto we've lived by throughout the season," said Hayes ahead of their date with destiny on the last day.

Well, that "mistake" was well and truly put to bed over the course of an incredible season in which we set an unrelenting pace from the very first whistle, with a squad put together by Hayes that seemed to have a little bit of everything.

The spine of the team started with Hedvig Lindahl in goal, as safe a pair of hands as could be found in the league, with Niamh Fahey and Gilly Flaherty rekindling the dominant centre-back pairing they had developed at Arsenal. Katie Chapman was another ex-Gunner who brought combativeness and a never-say-die attitude, while Eni Aluko's pace up top allowed us to stretch teams to their limit. Throw in homegrown talents Drew Spence and Hannah Blundell, fans' favourite Claire Rafferty and a young Millie Bright, and we could cope with almost anything thrown at us.

Any great side needs that X-Factor, though, and in Ji So-Yun and Gemma Davison, we certainly had that. Ji could unlock any defence and had a knack for popping up with vital goals and Davison was a jinking winger who got fans off their seats. Fran Kirby's mid-season arrival from Reading was just the icing on the cake.

After a brilliant campaign, it all came down to the final day, when we hosted Sunderland at our former home of Wheatsheaf Park, attended by 2,710 raucous supporters, which included men's team captain John Terry. Ji's early goal settled the nerves and then Kirby scored twice, Davison added a fourth and another devastating attacking display had taken us to the promised land.

No one could dispute the best team was crowned champions, as we led the table for nearly the entire season, scored the most goals and conceded the fewest. Off the field, the average attendance at Wheatsheaf Park rose by an incredible 164 per cent compared to the previous season, which was an early indication of just how much the women's game was growing – and that upward trajectory has continued ever since.

It truly was the start of something beautiful, and we've been counting the trophies ever since...

History Makers

HEDVIG LINDAHL
Ultra reliable Swedish goalkeeper who spent four years as a Blue and was a major force on the international stage too.

HANNAH BLUNDELL
Came through the ranks to become a serial trophy winner, playing in either full-back position, before leaving for Manchester United in 2021.

GILLY FLAHERTY
Known as 'Ledge' at Kingsmeadow, this hard-as-nails centre-half always led by example and is now a co-commentator for various WSL broadcasters in the UK.

NIAMH FAHEY
Veteran Republic of Ireland defender who brought a winning mentality from her time at Arsenal and helped us to the best defensive record in the league.

CLAIRE RAFFERTY
Only injuries prevented Raff from winning more caps as England's left-back, but her decade-long stay as a Blue made her a legend at the club.

KATIE CHAPMAN
Chappers won her first FA Cup as a 14-year-old and just kept lifting silverware right up to her retirement in 2018, captaining Chelsea to our first major honours.

MILLIE BRIGHT
Joined us from Donny ahead of the 2015 season and has developed into one of the very best in the world, winning trophies galore with us and captaining England in a World Cup final.

DREW SPENCE
Homegrown midfielder with a silky-smooth technique and as tough as they come. Even a move to Tottenham hasn't dented her reputation as a Blues legend!

JI SO-YUN
Perhaps the most important foreign import in WSL history. Ji came to us in 2015 and delighted supporters up and down the country, scoring some outrageous goals along the way.

GEMMA DAVISON
Undoubtedly the WSL's best winger during the early years of the league, which she won with Arsenal, Liverpool and Chelsea. Ghosted past players as if they weren't even there!

FRAN KIRBY
Joined us as 'Mini Messi' and left nine years later with an unbelievable tally of team and individual honours, as well as scoring more goals for the Blues than any other player in the modern era.

ENIOLA ALUKO
Before Kirby, Aluko held our goal record, which she accrued across two spells with the club, and she also won the WSL Golden Boot during her illustrious time as a Blue.

MILLIE BRIGHT

CONTINENTAL
Celebrations

It was a busy summer for some of our European and South American players in 2024 – but ultimately one that ended in success for two Blues...

CUCU COMES UP TRUMPS

Marc Cucurella became the third Spaniard to win the European Championship as a Chelsea player and, to cap it all off, our left-back was included in the Euro 2024 Team of the Tournament.

It's fair to say that Cucu might not have been expecting the summer to have panned out quite how it did, considering that he'd only played three times for his country leading up to Germany '24, and Spain weren't among the pre-tournament favourites.

But they were undoubtedly the best side over the course of the competition, with Cucurella key to their performances as he started six of their seven games and thrived down the left-hand side in tandem with Nico Williams.

Cucu helped his side past some of the biggest countries in Europe, as they saw off Italy, Germany, France and then England in the final. He saved his best moment until last in a tense finale against the Three Lions. With just four minutes remaining, he delivered a teasing low cross that Mikel Oyarzabal turned past Jordan Pickford and into the net to win Euro 2024. It was some way for Cucurella to register his first assist for Spain, and a fitting denouement to a spectacular tournament for our left-back.

ARGENTINA DOUBLE UP

After winning the World Cup in 2022, Argentina and Enzo Fernandez added the Copa America, meaning our midfielder has won both of the senior international tournaments he has taken part in!

Before the tournament in the USA, Argentina were hoping to win the trophy for the 16th time, which is more than any other nation, and Enzo was one of the mainstays in their team as he appeared in five matches, including the final against Colombia. A goal from Inter Milan striker Lautaro Martinez was enough to see them past their rivals, and Enzo will now be hoping for silverware at club level to add to his impressive medal collection on the international stage.

Moises Caicedo was the other Chelsea player involved in the Copa America, representing Ecuador at the tournament. They reached the quarter-final but were beaten by the eventual winners Argentina after a penalty shootout.

PALMER WRITES HISTORY

Euro 2024 might not have finished quite how our England duo of Cole Palmer and Conor Gallagher had hoped, but there was a little bit of history created for Chelsea thanks to the former's goal in the final.

Coming off the bench, as he did for each of his five appearances at the tournament, Palmer curled home a wonderful strike from outside the box to draw England level against Spain. Although it wasn't to be for the Three Lions, it was a third goal in a Euros final by a Chelsea player, which is more than any other club has managed! He joins Juan Mata and Fernando Torres, who were both on target for Spain against Italy in 2012, shortly after winning the Champions League with the Blues.

WHO ELSE WAS THERE?

Overall there were eight players representing Chelsea at the Euros, although for several of them the tournament ended at the group stage. Djordje Petrovic was unused by Serbia as they went out early, while Armando Broja and Mykhailo Mudryk made two appearances for Albania and Ukraine respectively as they also failed to make the knockout stages. Romelu Lukaku went goalless in four matches for Belgium, who were eliminated in the last 16, and Ian Maatsen didn't make an appearance for the Netherlands in their run to the semi-finals – although he was only a Chelsea player during the group stage as he signed for Aston Villa halfway through the tournament.

TEEN DREAMS

Chelsea lost our youngest-ever goalscorer in 2024 when Ian 'Chico' Hamilton passed away. We take a look back at Chico and all the other teenage heroes at Stamford Bridge...

SWEET SIXTEEN

Ian Hamilton was aged 16 years and 138 days when he made his debut for Chelsea's first team, which made him our youngest-ever player. He was called into the side for a London derby away at Tottenham in March 1967, and he made sure his name was double-stamped in the record books when he headed in Chelsea's equaliser in a 1-1 draw. That made him our youngest-ever goalscorer too.

His nickname was 'Chico', because there was a jazz artist at the time known as Chico Hamilton. He went on to play five games for us, scoring twice, before he moved to Southend United in 1968. He later made his name at Aston Villa, where his manager was Tommy Docherty, the man who gave him his debut at Chelsea.

YOUNGEST BLUES

'Chico' Hamilton remains the youngest man to play for Chelsea, but five others have also played for the Blues at the age of 16. Here are the youngest 10 players to appear for Chelsea's men's team:

Player	Debut	Age
Ian Hamilton	18/3/1967	16y 138d
Kingsley Whiffen	9/5/1967	16y 157d
Tommy Langley	9/11/1974	16y 274d
Michael Woods	6/1/2007	16y 275d
John Sparrow	13/3/1974	16y 238d
Mike Harrison	13/4/1957	16y 360d
Ian Pearce	11/5/1991	17y 4d
Ethan Ampadu	20/9/2017	17y 6d
Brian Bason	16/9/1972	17y 13d

TEENS ON TARGET

Hamilton also still holds the record as our youngest-ever goalscorer, but here are a couple of other teenage talents to have made their way into the club's history books with their exploits in front of goal.

YOUNGEST GOALSCORER IN EUROPEAN COMPETITION
Callum Hudson-Odoi
18 years, 22 days (v PAOK, Europa League, 29/11/2018)

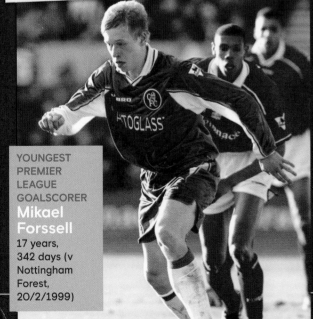

YOUNGEST PREMIER LEAGUE GOALSCORER
Mikael Forssell
17 years, 342 days (v Nottingham Forest, 20/2/1999)

JODY MORRIS:
FOREVER YOUNG

Jody Morris is currently Chelsea's youngest Premier League debutant. He was aged 17 years and 44 days when he came on as a substitute for John Spencer in a 5-0 win over Middlesbrough at Stamford Bridge on 4 February 1996.

The Premier League was created in 1992 and keeps its own records for events since that year, but when 'Chico' Hamilton made his debut at a younger age, the top flight in English football was called the First Division.

Morris returned to Chelsea after he retired as a player, and became an Academy coach here, winning the FA Youth Cup and the Under-18 Premier League twice each. He inspired many a young Blues fan when he burst onto the scene as a teenage midfield marvel, and then did the same as a coach years later. The fact that Jody was a Chelsea fan, who grew up down the road from Stamford Bridge, was the icing on the cake!

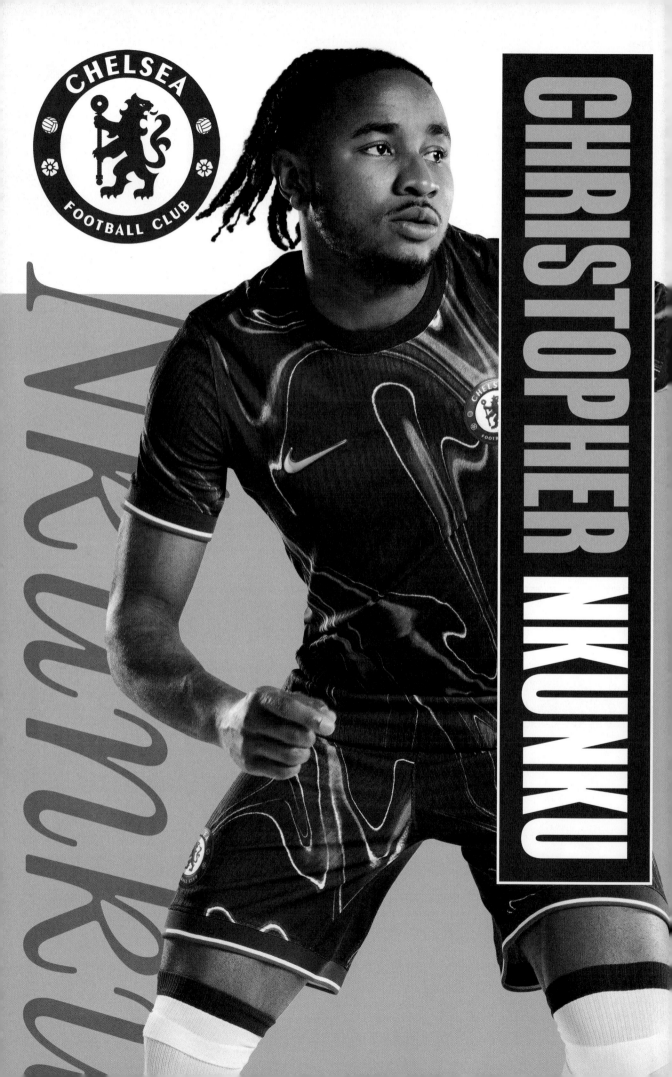

SOCCER AID 2024

The annual Soccer Aid for UNICEF fixture was held at Stamford Bridge last summer, featuring a mixture of celebrities and football legends – including a few Chelsea favourites – and it didn't disappoint...

WHAT IS SOCCER AID?

Stamford Bridge opened its doors for a very special fixture in June, as our west-London home hosted Soccer Aid for the 14th edition of a match which brings together a selection of footballing greats and celebrities for an England versus a World XI fixture. All in the name of charity, the annual event was the brainchild of pop superstar Robbie Williams and has been running since 2006. It aims to bring the nation together to help children worldwide have the best possible start in life and has raised more than £100 million since its inception.

WHICH CHELSEA LEGENDS WERE INVOLVED?

This was the second time the game has been held at the Bridge, following on from a thrilling penalty shoot-out win for the World XI in 2019, and the stadium was packed out to see some legendary players from our past once again running out on a pitch where they enjoyed some incredible moments during their peak years.

No less than five of the squad from our victorious 2012 Champions League final were in the two squads, with Petr Cech, Michael Essien and John Mikel Obi in the World XI camp, and Ashley Cole and Gary Cahill lining up for England. On top of that, the Three Lions could call upon Joe Cole, Karen Carney and Ellen White, while the world side had arguably the star attraction of the whole event: Eden Hazard. Five years after we said goodbye to the brilliant Belgian, he was back to light up the Bridge once more.

The Chelsea involvement didn't end there, either. Both managers had recently enjoyed spells in charge of the Blues, with Frank Lampard and Mauricio Pochettino coming up against each other.

STORY OF THE GAME

There was end-to-end action throughout an absorbing 90 minutes, and it was Joe Cole who set the tone for a goal-filled contest by controlling a ball on his chest and firing through the legs of his former team-mate Cech.

Hazard added to his collection of highlight-reel moments at the Bridge by curling home a free-kick past David James, while another ex-Blue was on target after the World XI had taken the lead, as White made history by becoming the first female goalscorer in Soccer Aid history.

The game was evenly poised at 2-2 going into the half-time break, but the introduction of celebrity goalkeepers meant it was raining goals after the break. Entrepreneur Steven Bartlett scored twice either side of a Jermain Defoe strike to put England in control, and though the World XI pulled one back through a penalty from football freestyler Billy Wingrove, Theo Walcott netted his side's sixth to ensure England won the trophy for the first time since 2018.

But the most important contribution of the night arguably came after the final whistle when Soccer Aid founder Williams informed the crowd that the 2024 event had raised £15,049,590 for UNICEF, taking the total since 2006 to more than £106 million.

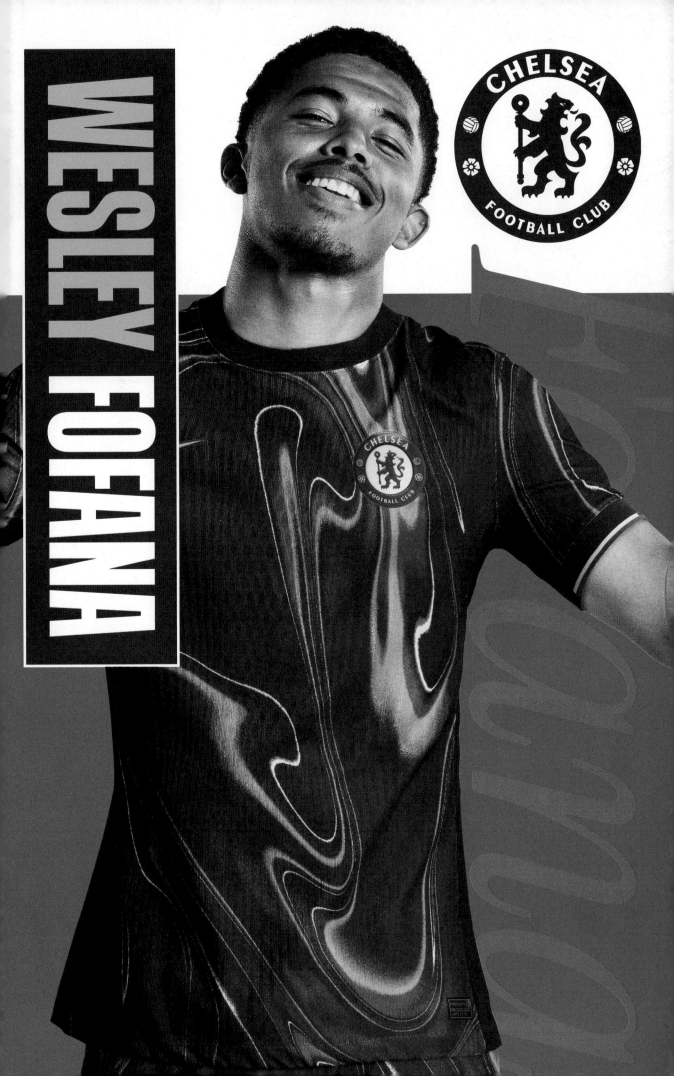

WESLEY FOFANA

CHELSEA FOOTBALL CLUB

24 25

AWAY KIT

CFC LDN

SHOP ONLINE AT CHELSEAMEGASTORE.COM
OR VISIT US IN THE STADIUM MEGASTORE

MAYRA RAMIREZ

1955, 2005 OR 2015?

Chelsea are celebrating the anniversary of three of our six top-flight titles this season. Here are a series of statements relating to each of those triumphs – your job is to assign it to the correct year

2 Jose Mourinho was our manager for two of these titles, but it was another coach, Ted Drake, who was in charge of us in this season to remember.

- ☐ 1955
- ☐ 2005
- ☐ 2015

1 Chelsea recorded a points tally of 95, which is the most we've ever got in a single top-flight season.

☐ 1955   ☐ 2005   ☐ 2015

3 We set a new English top-flight record of conceding only 15 times in our 38 league matches in this season!

☐ 1955   ☐ 2005   ☐ 2015

4 Eden Hazard scored the goal against Crystal Palace that clinched the title.

☐ 1955   ☐ 2005   ☐ 2015

1ST

2ND

6 Wolverhampton Wanderers finished second behind the title-winning Blues.

☐ 1955 ☐ 2005 ☐ 2015

5 We only lost one league game all season, when Nicolas Anelka – who would later sign for Chelsea – scored the only goal in a 1–0 defeat against Manchester City.

☐ 1955 ☐ 2005 ☐ 2015

8 Cesc Fabregas led the team in terms of assists as he won his first English title, having failed to do so during his time at Arsenal.

☐ 1955 ☐ 2005 ☐ 2015

7 Diego Costa was our leading scorer in the league, scoring 20 times in his first season with the club after signing from Atletico Madrid.

☐ 1955 ☐ 2005 ☐ 2015

9 Chelsea Football Club celebrated its 100th birthday just a couple of months before winning this title.

☐ 1955
☐ 2005
☐ 2015

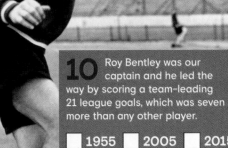

10 Roy Bentley was our captain and he led the way by scoring a team-leading 21 league goals, which was seven more than any other player.

☐ 1955 ☐ 2005 ☐ 2015

FEEL
what they *felt*

2005, Drogba scores in the Quarter-Final of the UEFA Champions League. Stamford Bridge, London.

BOOK NOW:

MUSEUM
& TOURS

History you can *feel*